BILLIE EILISH

Written by Sally Morgan © Scholastic Children's Books

Copyright © 2019 by Scholastic Inc.

ISBN 978-1-338-63066-4

10 9 8 7 6 5 4 3 2   20 21 22 23

Printed in the U.S.A.   40

First edition, 2020

BILLIE EILISH

100% unofficial

the
ultimate
unofficial
fanbook

contents

everything you need to know about the queen of pop!

INTRODUCTION

"call me friend but keep me closer"

Billie Eilish is the future. Since she released her debut single "Ocean Eyes" on SoundCloud in 2015, she has become one of the most streamed artists on the planet. From her unique sound to her statement style, Billie is one of a kind, and she looks set to dominate the music industry for many years to come.

As well as discovering tons of facts about Billie, from her musical influences and love of hip-hop to the inspiration behind some of your favorite songs, this book has pages for you to record information about your own dreams and write powerful lyrics.

#followme

Billie is on all major social media platforms.

You can follow her via @billieeilish on Instagram, @billieeilish on Twitter, and billie-eilish on Snapchat.

STAY SAFE

Instagram, YouTube, and other platforms can be loads of fun, and a great way to stay in touch with your friends and ultimate idols—but always make sure to stay safe online. Never give away your full name, address, phone number, or details of your school. Don't post photos that might give away the location of your home or school. If somebody is leaving comments that make you uncomfortable, talk to an adult.

do what you love

If something is going to be a career, you have to spend a lot of time doing it—so think carefully about what your ambition is and DON'T do something just because your fave celeb does it. It's great to be inspired but your talent needs to come from the heart, too!

get comfortable in front of a crowd

Billie says, "It's really fun to be on stage in front of people." If a big crowd sounds terrifying to you, try performing in front of a smaller group of people, maybe just your parents and your friends, then slowly work your way up to a bigger audience.

practice makes perfect

If you want to succeed, you have to be prepared to work hard at your talent—and practice regularly, even if this sometimes means missing out on a trip to the movies with your friends or cutting down on your YouTube time. However, it's equally important not to work too hard—fun with your friends is healthy, so make sure you leave SOME time for those trips to the movies!

banish the nerves

Even the biggest stars can suffer from stage fright—it's natural, and just a reminder that whatever you are about to do means a lot to you. So whether you are preparing for a school talent show or your first ever audition, remember to take some deep breaths beforehand and remind yourself that even Billie felt like this once! Ask yourself, what's the worst that can happen? Even if things go wrong this time, there will be other opportunities in the future—so you might as well go for it!

#idontwannabeyouanymore

DREAMING OF A FUTURE IN THE SPOTLIGHT LIKE BILLIE? TALENT WILL ONLY TAKE YOU SO FAR—HARD WORK AND DEDICATION ARE WHAT REALLY GOT HER TO THE TOP. HERE ARE SOME TIPS FOR MAKING IT.

listen to feedback

It's important to get feedback so that you can continue to strengthen your skill. Whether it's from a singing coach or even your mom, ask someone to give you notes on what you are doing well and what you could be doing better. And be prepared to listen to their advice. Even though it can be hard to hear that you're not doing things perfectly—yet! —it's something every star needs to hear a lot in their career so that they can work out how to keep getting better.

stay true to you

The music world can be tough and you can face rejection or criticism. And if you're posting content online, it can be easy to get caught up in negative comments. But if you stay positive and give out confident vibes, good things will come your way. Give it a hundred percent and always channel your inner Billie—work hard, believe in yourself, and have fun!

all about BILLIE EILISH

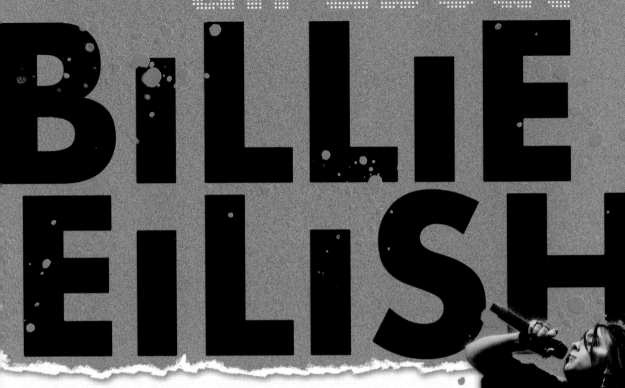

While growing up, Billie saw her older brother, Finneas O'Connell, fall in love with music. Additionally, her mother wrote songs and her father played instruments such as the piano and the ukulele. The musical vibe in the house inspired little Billie to make a career in music.

On top of her other talents, Billie has her own unique style. She wears her signature oversized skater gear and has said, "I always wear the kind of stuff that makes you overheat and die."

NAME: Billie Eilish Pirate Baird O'Connell
SINGER NAME: Billie Eilish
DATE OF BIRTH: DECEMBER 18, 2001
STAR SIGN: Sagittarius
BORN IN: Los Angeles, California
FAMOUS AS: Singer-songwriter

Billie has always loved music! She is an American singer and songwriter. She joined a choir at the age of eight, and by the time she turned eleven, she had begun writing and singing her own songs. Finneas was the biggest influence in her life while she was growing up. He had his own band and had written a song called "Ocean Eyes." Billie performed the song and released it online. It became a massive success and turned out to be her first breakthrough.

"i've always done whatever i want and always been exactly who i am."

the bad girl of pop

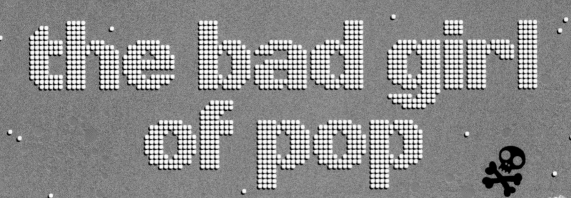

Today, it seems as though Billie Eilish is everywhere. Her haunting melodies stream from every device, reaction vids and stories fill your feed and her signature style influence the fashion choices of men and women more than twice her age. She is a musical sensation, a style icon and an influencer beyond compare with more celebrity fans than she has items of designer clothing (which is a lot), but where did she come from? Looking at Billie's career from the surface it would be easy to assume that this goth-pop princess won some kind of lottery when she bounced from her brother's bedroom-based music studio and straight up into the stratosphere of superstardom, but is her success really an overnight stroke of luck that could happen to anyone, or is this tormented and talented teen reaping the rewards of years of hard work? Read on to untangle the myths from this music legend.

A STAR IS BORN

Billie was born on the 18 December 2001 in Los Angeles, California to parents Maggie Baird and Patrick O'Connell.

Billie's parents weren't your average parents, there is a clue to this if you take a closer look at Billie's full name:

billie eilish pirate baird o'connell

How many Pirates do you know? Eilish is a Gaelic/Irish derivative of Elizabeth and Baird is her mother's last name.

From Billie's name, it is clear that her parents were very creative people, which probably comes in very handy given that they are both professional performers.

Billie's mother, Maggie Baird is a singer, songwriter, screenwriter and an actor. Maggie is best known for her role in the film she co-wrote and starred in named *Life Inside Out* and her voice work in *Mass Effect 2* – and for being Billie's mum, of course.

Billie's dad, Patrick O'Connell, starred in films such as *Iron Man* and *Supergirl* as well as the TV programme, *The West Wing*. Billie's father is a talented musician and plays many instruments including the ukulele but is also probably best known for being Billie's dad. Hooray for Billie!

> "me and my dad are very, very similar."
>
> – Billie Eilish on her dad

> "i love her take on the world. she's always said and done interesting things."
>
> – Billie's dad on Billie

Clearly, Billie was born into a house where expressing yourself artistically was seen as normal and unremarkable as brushing your teeth. Luckily, growing up, Billie found she loved to perform, just like her parents and her older brother, Finneas. Phew!

LITTLE VOICE

> "i never really started singing, i was always just singing or making noise, always yelling, always listening to music, so music has never really been like a thought like 'maybe i should pursue music', because i'm already doing that."
>
> – Billie Eilish

The world was blown away by Billie's voice after the release of 'Ocean Eyes' in 2015, but people who were close to Billie knew Billie was a singer from when she was very little. In fact, Billie wrote her first song when she was just four years old. Wow!

Billie loved to sing, but unlike the confident moshing performer you see onstage today, young(er) Billie was very shy and would often perform songs for her family and friends from behind a pillow. Bless!

Even though she was shy, Billie found the courage to perform in her first talent show when she was six years old, singing a Beatles song named, 'Happiness is a Warm Gun'. Perhaps not the most obvious choice for a young girl, but even then, nothing about Billie was.

Billie loved all different kinds of music partly thanks to her father, Patrick, who would make her and her brother mixtapes of some of his favourite music including everything from classic bands such as the Beatles to the punky pop of Avril Lavigne. As well as listening to music and singing, Finneas and Billie learned how to play all different instruments from the piano to the ukulele.

CHOIR GIRL

As well as performing for family and in talent shows, Billie got the chance to explore her love of music at eight years old, when she followed her brother singing for the Los Angeles Children's Chorus (LACC).

The Los Angeles Children's Chorus uniform of a red wool tank top, white blouse and black tie may seem like a far cry from the 'wonky' style she is known for today, but Billie felt right at home. In the choir she found herself surrounded by friends who loved to perform as much as she did. With the choir, Billie sang all different types of

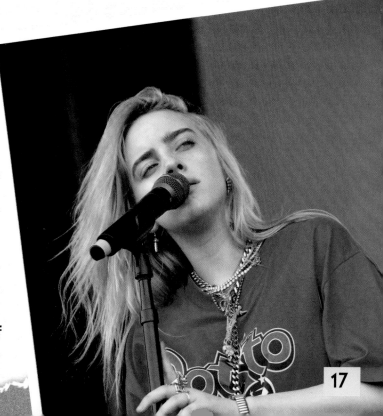

music from pop and gospel to classical and learned how to use her voice properly.

Billie loved to perform alongside her friends, but she didn't discover that performing on stage solo was what really she wanted until she was twelve, when she went to see a performance of the musical 'Matilda'. Billie watched the performance transfixed and when the actress came out to take her bow and the audience erupted in applause, Billie knew for certain that was what she wanted to do. To stand on a stage and to have everyone look at her and applaud. She wanted to connect with an audience. Even though Billie was only twelve at the time, she was worried that she was already too late.

CENTRE STAGE

Billie might be famous for singing, but her real love growing up was dance. Billie loved to dance and dreamed of one day becoming a professional dancer. Like everything Billie was always passionate about, she worked hard at it, spending up to eleven hours a week in the dance studio rehearsing and competing as part of a company. Billie loved to use her body to express herself and she was good at it.

Billie was an excellent

LA

dancer and would often rehearse with girls older than herself. In 2015, while Billie was rehearsing a hip-hop routine with senior dancers, Billie suffered something called a growth-plate injury. A bone separated from her muscle in her hip. It was very painful, but worse than that, her dreams of becoming a professional dancer were dashed. Had all those hours in the dance studio been for nothing?

Far from it. Anyone watching one of Billie's videos or seeing her perform live on stage can see what a talented dancer she is and although it may appear that her movements are random and natural they are much more than that. They are instinctive movements of a dancer who has trained hard to know how to control her movements and express herself to music.

DANCE WITH DESTINY

Dance has played an enormous part in Billie's life, not only because of her dreams of being a dancer, but also because it was creating a track for herself to dance to that gave Billie her big break. Her teacher, knowing Billie was a great singer, asked her to record a song that they could choreograph a dance to. Billie agreed and roped her brother in to help. Sitting cross-legged on her brother's bed, with Finneas at the computer, Billie laid down 'Ocean Eyes', a song Finneas had written to perform with his band, The Slightlys.

They uploaded the song to the audio sharing platform, SoundCloud, for Billie's teacher to hear but soon discovered that it had been played more than 1,000 times, then 10,000. The song was going viral. Gathering fans and followers at a fast pace, a few months later Billie would sign with boutique label, Dark

Room and would release her first EP 'Don't Smile at Me'.

"it's never seemed unbelievable to me because i just think she is so talented."
— Finneas O'Connell

A GREAT TEAM

Even though Billie's songs have been streamed more than one billion times and have broken records on Spotify and Apple Music, Billie still records most of them sitting cross-legged on her brother's bed, with him at his computer. She feels this gives the songs their intimacy and also allows them a lot more creative freedom than if they were working in a studio. This way they can be in control of what they produce which is something Billie is passionate about.

TOO COOL FOR SCHOOL

With all her time devoted to dance and choir and now meteoric fame, you might be wondering when Billie and Finneas found the time to go to school. Come to think of it, a quick scan of Billie's Instagram shows that even though she is just seventeen years old, Billie doesn't look much like an average school girl and that may be because she never was one.

Billie's parents decided that mainstream school wasn't where Finneas and Billie would reach their true potential. They wanted to give their children the chance to discover what they were passionate about for themselves, so that working hard to do well wouldn't feel like something they were forced to do.

Instead of maths and physics lessons, Maggie and Patrick surrounded their children with everything they needed to learn what they wanted – books, musical instruments, equipment and the opportunity to find out more about what they wanted to know from other people.

Some might think that home school is an excuse to skive off working, but if Billie and Finneas were hoping to spend their days playing video games and raiding the refrigerator they were out of luck.

Billie's parents expected their kids to work hard and put in the hours to achieve their goals, but they hoped giving them control of what they worked hard at would make things seem a lot easier. It appears to have paid off. Finneas has the words '10,000 hours' written above his doorframe which can be seen from his bed, referring to the theory that you have to spend 10,000 hours focussing on and practising something in order to become world class at it.

If Billie wasn't drumming her fingers on her desk in maths lessons, what did she spend her time learning? Whatever she wanted to. Billie was in control of what she wanted to study and how she wanted to study it.

One lesson they both enjoyed was song-writing with their mother Maggie. Maggie encouraged her children to transform their feelings into songs. She taught them that inspiration was all around them and this is something Billie took to heart writing one of her first songs about something she saw in one of her favourite TV shows at the time *The Walking Dead.*

Home school would seem to have been the right choice for this talented pair. Billie and Finneas may not have spent as much time studying maths as their peers, but what they did learn seems to have added up nicely.

HOME LIFE

You might think having actors for parents would be rather glamorous, but life as an artist and a performer can be unpredictable and Billie's parents were not wealthy. Billie says the neighbourhood she grew up in wasn't exactly dangerous, but her neighbours were arrested for laundering money. She also claims to have heard gunshots from time to time.

Billie's house was comfortable but it wasn't large. With only two bedrooms, Billie's parents allowed each of their children to have their own bedrooms, while they slept on a futon in the living room.

BILLIE'S ROOM

Even now, Billie loves her room and likes nothing more than getting back from touring and sleeping in her own bed and using her own bathroom. Billie has really made her room an expression of who she is, writing her thoughts and feelings on one of the walls (another sign Maggie and Patrick aren't your average parents – most would flip). What she writes is very personal to her though so she covers the wall with a Louis Vuitton blanket and only allows her very closest friends to see what is written there.

As well as writing on her wall, Billie also keeps a notebook where she writes all of her ideas for songs and lyrics. Billie used to take this notebook everywhere she went until she accidentally left it behind after a gig in Germany. Billie had to get someone from the record company to pick it up and to send it securely back to her home in LA where she says it is now safely stashed in her room.

FAMILY LIFE

Growing up, everyone was busy on various projects rushing here and there for auditions, filming and recording sessions, as well as all kinds of classes. Billie's mum, Maggie, says they weren't the typical LA family because whenever they could they got together to share a family meal. Billie says her mum does most of the cooking. Her favourite things her mum cooks? Mashed potatoes and gravy.

Billie loves food and according to her blog became a vegan in 2014 which means she tries not to eat or use animal products. Billie says she did this to reduce her impact on the environment as well as to do less harm to animals.

Aside from mashed potatoes and gravy (vegan of course), Billie says she loves spicy foods such as vegan hot wings and spicy tofu. She also loves chips and guacamole and insists on travelling with her favourite brand of refried beans whenever she is on tour.

If Billie could be any food she thinks she would be a burrito because she says she has eaten so many of them.

DARK LIFE

Billie's comfortable home, supportive family and abundance of opportunities to express herself isn't exactly what you expect to hear about a girl who sings songs about killing her friends or being beaten up by men or who can be seen in her music videos drinking poison or having needles driven into her naked back. So where does this darkness come from?

> **"you don't have to be in love to write a song about being in love and you don't have to hate someone to write a song about hating someone, it's just fun to put yourself in a place that you would not be otherwise."**
>
> – Billie Eilish

Billie doesn't believe you have to have experienced things in order to be able to sing about them. For instance, she never has sat in the front of her car chewing gum with her dead friends in the boot. Phew! That being said, Billie does insist on doing her own stunts in her music videos wherever possible. She may not have murdered any of her friends, but she has had a large spider climb out of her mouth! Yuck!

LOVE LIFE

Billie has claimed that she has never been in love before, but she has freely admitted that she has had one romantic love in her life – Justin Bieber.

Billie says she would cry over the fact that even though she loved him and thought of herself as 'Billie Bieber', Justin didn't know she existed. To Justin she was nothing more than just another fan.

Billie had said in many interviews that she never wanted to meet Justin, and was scared out of her mind when Ellen DeGeneres surprised her with a Bieber lookalike when she appeared on her show in early 2019. EEK!

Billie may have loved Justin from afar, while he had no idea who she was, but he knows who she is now – he would have to be living under a rock not to. Like over 20 million others, Justin follows Billie on Instagram and has even sent her DMs of the messages she sent him when she was a young fan.

If Billie was really terrified of meeting Justin, it didn't show at the Coachella festival in 2019 where they not only met, but danced together to music by performed by Ariana Grande and NSYNC.

FAN LIFE

Loving music as Billie does meant she went to lots of shows growing up and Billie loves to be in the audience almost as much as she loves being on stage. Billie says she likes to dance right at the front in the mosh pit. Jumping and dancing in the mosh pit means she is as close to the performer as possible and she is living the music, but things can get pretty rough. Billie has said that she has even been punched in the face.

From going to gigs and her love for Justin Bieber, Billie knows what it's like to be a fan, which is why she says she performs like she is down at the front in the pit with hers. She describes her shows as feeling like karaoke nights where she doesn't really need to sing due to the thousands of voices all ready and willing to provide her vocal. One of the first times Billie remembers hearing someone sing her songs back to her was in 2016 when she was at a late slot that only ten people showed up to. To her delight, two of the girls in the audience sang back to her. Billie said this made her cry then and still does. Even when it is tens of thousands of people who probably can't even hear her over themselves. Whether she is performing to 10 people or 10,000 people, Billie does her best to put on a great show for her fans.

> "i want to be as reachable as i can for them, as equal, because nobody is on a higher pedestal. i'm not higher than they are ... we're all on this same level and we're all the same age. that's what's so interesting."
>
> – Billie Eilish

GETTING SOCIAL

One of the things Billie says she is proudest of is her fanbase. She feels like they are like a family to her and social media is the perfect way for her to connect with them and let them know what she is doing. Billie shares a lot online and uploads stories and live streams regularly. Billie does her best to interact with fans by liking their posts, sharing them and writing back to them whenever she can.

Billie even gets some of her ideas from her fans. In the video for 'When the Party's Over', Billie looks directly into the camera as she drinks a noxious looking black liquid which can later be seen streaming down from her eyes as inky black tears.

Billie claims that a drawing she was sent by a fan in Montreal inspired her. The picture was of herself crying black inky tears. Billie says she thanked the fan who sent her more art which gave her even more ideas. Like her music, Billie is in control of her own social media, taking time to consider what she posts and how it contributes to her image.

"instagram is how i show what i think is cool. i never post about my music, it's more this is what i was wearing here, look at how weird it is."

— Billie Eilish

PERSONAL LIFE

Billie says she used to feel she had to share everything online, but is learning to find a balance. She says she likes knowing that there are things that hardly anyone knows about her, but sometimes she feels that she doesn't have a choice.

In November 2018, Billie opened up about a condition that had affected her her entire life. After a series of videos taken from interview outtakes showed Billie rolling her eyes and making faces some viewers thought odd, rather than let people make up their own stories about what was happening, she decided to share her own story. Billie confirmed that she lives with a neurological condition known as Tourette Syndrome.

Tourette Syndrome can cause involuntary movements, known as tics, in someone who lives with the condition and in some cases, can cause people to shout unwanted words or sounds. Billie has learned to live with her condition, but one of the ways she controls it is using her time that she thinks she is off camera in an interview.

In an Instagram post Billie said, "It's something I grew up with and am used to ... my family and closest friends know it as a part of me."

Since opening up about her Tourettes, Billie has discovered that many of her fans live with the same condition. She says it makes her feel at home to know so many others have had a similar experience and she feels glad that she can be a role model for people who have the condition.

GOING GLOBAL

As well as interacting with her fans online, like many artists, Billie spends a lot of her time on tour, performing in cities all over the world. Everywhere she goes she puts on a great show and she loves playing for her fans and connecting with them. From the surface these tours could look like one long party, and while Billie has fun a lot of the time, it can be hard. Long days of travel, countless interviews, screaming fans all wanting to get close to her. To help, Billie's mother and brother often go on tour with her but even then it can feel lonely being away from your friends for so long.

Billie has said that being on tour can make her feel isolated. She feels that being away can lead to some of her friends moving on without her. She understands but she still finds it hard. Not many of her friends can understand the experience she has had. They are all getting jobs and getting ready for college and deciding what they want to do with their lives. Billie feels like she already knows what she wants to do with her life. She has her career.

> **"i never don't know what i want, i always know what i want and how i want it."**
>
> – Billie Eilish

Billie has gone from singing in her brother's bedroom to global superstar in such a short time that it is hard to imagine where she will go next. Her music has broken records, she has performed sell-out tours and has millions of followers. In April 2019, Billie released her first album, *When We All Fall Asleep, Where Do We Go?* Her fans and the critics loved it. The album debuted at number 1 on the Billboard Hot 200 list and 12 of the tracks from the 13 track album made the Hot 100, making Billie the first woman in the 60 year history of the list to have 14 tracks in the list at the same time (including her song 'Lovely').

WHAT HAPPENS NEXT ...

One of the reasons it is hard to predict what Billie will do next is because Billie is unlike any star that has come before. Billie's career is on her terms and has been from the very beginning. Unlike teen pop sensations of the past, from the moment she uploaded 'Ocean Eyes' Billie has been in charge of her music and her image. She had not been packaged by Disney or Nickelodeon, nor has she been painted and primped by a record company. In the past, stars had to be hugely famous to wrestle for control of their careers and music but Billie has had control from the very beginning and is determined to keep it. With her family at her side, she seems to have all the support she needs.

Billie plans to make more music both with her brother and in collaboration with other artists she admires. She also says she has plans to design her own fashion label to go hand-in-hand with the merchandise she has already produced. Billie considers herself a visual artist as much as a musician and loves to experiment with fashion, even making a shirt from an old IKEA bag. Whatever Billie does next, whether it be music, fashion or videos some have to watch from behind the sofa, she is in the driving seat for what will surely be a white-knuckle ride.

STRO
TOGE

NGER
THER

RISING UP, STAYING STRONG

Billie's talent and determination have rocketed her into the spotlight, but along the way people have helped her on the journey. It can be lonely at the top, but luckily Billie has family, friends, and fans supporting her success.

Growing up surrounded by a family of actors and musicians, Billie learned the importance of creativity and expression of art—she credits her wild imagination to her parents and musician brother. This close creative relationship is something the family continues to share and is an integral part of Billie's life and career.

Aware of the privilege of her position, Billie tries to remain true to herself and share her own unique perspective of the world through her lyrics and music. Billie's songs reflect themes that are related to the struggles teenagers face as they grow up in a society surrounded by the pressure to be perfect.

While growing up, Billie saw her brother, Finneas, fall in love with music. Her mother wrote songs and her father played instruments such as the piano and the ukulele. The musical vibe in the house inspired Billie to make a career in music.

From their childhood home in Los Angeles, Finneas co-wrote and produced his sister's haunting breakthrough "Ocean Eyes," which went viral on SoundCloud in 2015. It all started when one of Billie's teachers asked her if she or her brother could write a song that they could choreograph a dance to. Billie explained that "I was like, 'yes, that's such a cool thing to do!' Then, my brother came to me with "Ocean Eyes," which he had originally written for his band. He told me he thought it would sound really good in my voice. He taught me the song and we sang it together along to his guitar and I loved it—it was stuck in my head for weeks. We kind of just decided that that was the song we were going to use for the dance."

TRUE FANS

Billie has an extremely close relationship with her fans and she is constantly inspired by the support she receives. "I don't even call them fans. I don't like that. They're literally just a part of my life; they're a part of my family. I don't think of them as on a lower level than me. I don't think I'm anything but equal to all of them. So yeah, they're basically all of my siblings."

MUSE ON

"I listen to music all day every day. I can't not listen to music. It's kind of scary how much I listen to music, but it's what I love, and it's all I care about."

Billie has a ton of musical influences, from pop to hip-hop. Just like Billie, her favorite musicians and performers have their own unique style. "I like Tyler, the Creator a lot. He does anything he wants, really, and doesn't care if it works out or not, which I totally, completely admire. I also really like Earl Sweatshirt and Drake and Big Sean. Childish Gambino is also an incredible lyricist. I don't know how he does it. I love A$AP Rocky, Lana Del Rey, and Aurora."

Billie's family and their love for music also had a huge influence on her growing up. When she was young, her dad would make her mixtapes with a lot of different artists— Linkin Park, Avril Lavigne, The Beatles, Sarah McLachlan. Billie still loves Linkin Park and remains a huge fan of Chester Bennington. "I just really loved Linkin Park, and their production is really sick."

the real deal

"Being an artist doesn't just mean you have a song. That doesn't make you an artist. The word 'artist' means so many different things, and I feel like to be a real one, you really have to do it all. The people that I think of as artists—Tyler, the Creator, Childish Gambino, Kanye West—are doing the most." —Billie Eilish

pop princess

Billie is a different kind of pop star. She's one of a kind. Her hushed voice, baggy style, and dark lyrics subvert the norms of the "pop princess." Billie sees herself as challenging these norms, "I don't see myself as a pop artist. Like, when you hear 'pop,' you're like, 'Oh, bubblegum, jumpy little girly stuff,' and I feel like, 'Uh-uh. That's not me.'"

Today, Billie is changing the face of pop music. The gothic pop queen continues to carve out her own place in the music industry. Her moody melodies, horrorcore videos, and energetic performances inspire her fans around the world.

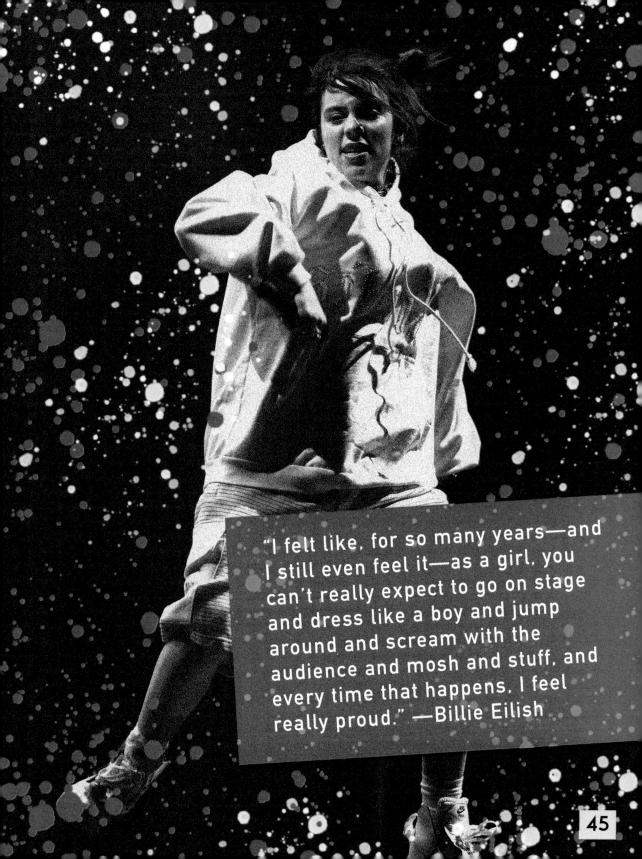

"I felt like, for so many years—and I still even feel it—as a girl, you can't really expect to go on stage and dress like a boy and jump around and scream with the audience and mosh and stuff, and every time that happens, I feel really proud." —Billie Eilish

FINNEAS O'CONNELL

Billie and her brother, Finneas, are extremely close. They worked together on Billie's debut album *When We All Fall Asleep, Where Do We Go?*, with Finneas both writing and producing alongside his sister.

NAME: Finneas O'Connell
SINGER NAME: FINNEAS
DATE OF BIRTH: JULY 30, 1997
STAR SIGN: Leo
BORN IN: Los Angeles, California
FAMOUS AS: Singer-songwriter and record producer
PERSONAL FACT: Finneas starred in the series *Glee* as the character Alistair.

Finneas had a passion for music at a young age and started writing and producing songs at the age of twelve. He then started his own band, The Slightlys, along with his friends.

In 2015, he co-wrote and produced his sister's breakthrough song "Ocean Eyes," which went viral on SoundCloud. Since then, Finneas has been working alongside Billie.

Finneas released his first solo single "New Girl" in 2016 and continues to build his own career as an artist. He has collaborated with dream-pop singer Ashe, along with R&B artist Sabrina Claudio and British singer-songwriter Bruno Major.

SIBLING RIVALRY

"Me and my brother get along super well. We're, like, best friends. So we'll stay up until, like, five just talking because we get along and, you know, it's cool. And he respects my opinions, and I respect his, even if we don't have the same opinions, but a lot of the time we do." —Billie Eilish

Don't smile at me !!

Raised by actor-musician parents, Finneas and Billie have become a formidable team in the music industry. Billie started writing songs at the age of eleven and has always loved making music with her brother. A musician himself, Finneas performs alongside his sister on both guitar and vocals.

From their childhood home in Los Angeles, Finneas co-wrote and produced his sister's haunting breakthrough "Ocean Eyes," which went viral on SoundCloud in 2015. He did the same for Eilish's EP *Don't Smile at Me* two years later, and has joined her backing band on worldwide tours and festival dates since.

Finneas has described the bond he has with his little sister as "unshakeable" and the two remain extremely close as they work alongside each other on Billie's musical projects.

KHALID

Billie Eilish and Khalid joined forces for a powerful single, "Lovely." Khalid first saw Billie perform when she was fifteen and he was blown away by her "star power." Their song is featured on the official soundtrack of the second season of *13 Reasons Why*.

Khalid's first single, "Location," was released in August 2016 when he was just eighteen. The song hit number two in the US R&B charts. Khalid has been compared to some amazing artists. including Frank Ocean, The Weekend, and Sampha. Frank Ocean and Chance the Rapper have inspired him, and he's also into pop acts like Lorde. But he says his biggest influence is his mother.

> "i was told i wasn't good enough, but i just chose not to listen."

NAME: Khalid Donnel Robinson
SINGER NAME: Khalid
DATE OF BIRTH: FEBRUARY 11, 1998
STAR SIGN: Aquarius
BORN IN: Fort Stewart, Georgia
FAMOUS AS: Singer-songwriter
PERSONAL FACT: His first name means 'eternal'

vince staples

Billie originally wrote "&burn" as a solo track, but once experimental hip-hop artist Vince Staples heard the song, he had to hop on. Billie has referred to Vince as being "a god." She said commenting during an interview that his work made him her top choice to feature on the song. "Vince Staples was my number one choice, so when we got him to hear it and he agreed to do, it was incredible," Billie said.

> I don't know who more confidently tries to do something or say something to change the communities more than rappers.
> —Vince Staples

Vince Staples was transformed by hip-hop at a young age. His inspirations include Kanye West, Lauryn Hill, Missy Elliott, and Andre 3000. Now a multi-talented artist, Vince is a rapper, singer, songwriter, and actor. He is part of the the hip-hop group Cutthroat Boyz alongside fellow rappers Aston Matthews and Joey Fatts.

Vince didn't have an easy life growing up in North Long Beach, but now he uses his celebrity to support local community programs. He understands the important position he's in to inspire young people with his music.

NAME: Vincent Jamal Staples
SINGER NAME: Vince Staples
DATE OF BIRTH: JULY 2, 1993
STAR SIGN: Cancer
BORN IN: North Long Beach, California
FAMOUS AS: Rapper, singer

PERSONAL FACT:

He collaborated with film composer Hans Zimmer on a remix of the UEFA Champions League Anthem for the FIFA 19 reveal trailer.

53

PERFECT PARTNER

1. I LIKE PEOPLE WHO ARE:
A) BUBBLY
B) ORGANIZED
C) CREATIVE

2. MY FAVE ACTIVITIES TO DO WITH MY FRIENDS ARE:
A) MAKING UP SONGS AND DANCE ROUTINES
B) SHARING STORIES AND CHILLING OUT TOGETHER
C) DISCOVERING NEW THINGS AND GOING ON ADVENTURES

3. IF ME AND MY FRIEND WERE SPENDING THE WEEKEND TOGETHER WE WOULD:
A) INVITE SOME PALS OVER AND HAVE A DANCE-OFF
B) HAVE A COZY NIGHT IN AND WATCH OUR FAVORITE MOVIES
C) DO SOMETHING CRAZY AND RANDOM

4. MY FRIEND GROUP IS MADE UP OF:
A) ANYONE WHO'S UP FOR HAVING FUN
B) ONE OR TWO VERY CLOSE PALS
C) LOTS OF FRIENDS WITH DIFFERENT INTERESTS

6. WHICH IS YOUR FAVORITE BILLIE SONG?
A) OCEAN EYES
B) LOVELY
C) COPYCAT

5. I LOVE MY BFF BECAUSE HE/SHE:
A) MAKES ME CRY WITH LAUGHTER
B) IS A REALLY GOOD LISTENER
C) IS ALWAYS THE LIFE AND SOUL OF THE PARTY

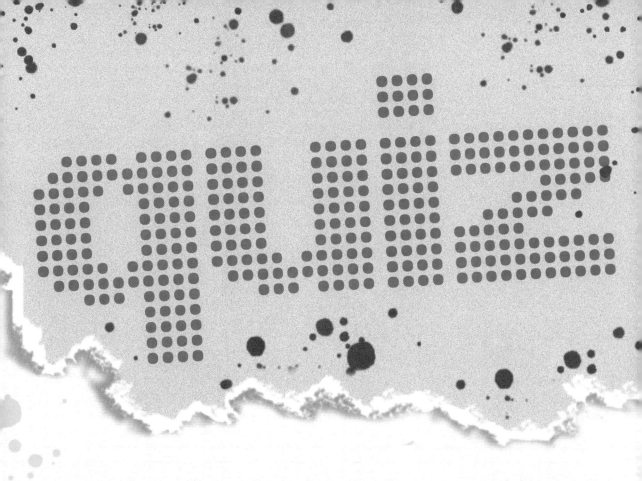

QUIZ

Mostly As: Your perfect pop partner is … Ariana Grande! Bubbly and fun-loving, this bow-obsessed girl is a laugh a minute. But don't be deceived—this pop sensation is an inspiring, uncompromising woman.

Mostly Bs: Your perfect pop partner is … Khalid! His kind and thoughtful personality means that his lyrics always have a deep meaning. He'll be there to encourage you creatively.

Mostly Cs: Your perfect pop partner is … Halsey! Outgoing and creative, she loves to surround herself with people. Her positive attitude to life makes her a real inspiration.

A

B

delve deeper

"WORDS ARE MORE POWERFUL THAN SOME NOISES. NOISES WON'T LAST LONG. LYRICS ARE SO IMPORTANT, AND PEOPLE DON'T REALIZE THAT." —BILLIE EILISH

Billie is able to express different emotions so vividly and visually through her music. And she manages to do so without being tied down to any specific genre. Whether you're feeling on top of the world, feeling like you're over relationships, or maybe feeling a little low, there's a Billie Eilish song that probably describes what you're going through.

"wish you were gay"

Have you ever been in love with someone who didn't feel that same way? Sometimes, no matter how hard you try, the person you like just ignores you. However, despite this, you can't help but be completely obsessed with them. This is a song about unrequited love for all the lonely hearts. It's reassuring to know that even Billie has been there. "I wrote this song about a guy that really was not interested in me and it made me feel horrible."

"lovely ft. khalid"

We can be our own worst enemies, and "lovely" relates to anyone who's ever felt alone in a crowded room. The title of the song contrasts with the low mood, but Billie has explained the reasoning behind this, "We called it [lovely] because the song was sort of really freaking depressing so then it's like 'oh, how lovely.' Just taking everything horrible like you know what this is great. I'm so happy being miserable."

"bellyache"

In life, we all do crazy things that we regret. "bellyache" takes this concept of guilt to the extreme. Billie has said that the lyrics come from the point of view of a person who has committed a murder and is struggling with that guilt. In an interview, Billie revealed more about the song: "'bellyache' is flat-out a song about murder. [. . .] That character [in the song] isn't me—but it also is. The song is really about doing terrible things and not really knowing [why]."

"you should see me in a crown"

Billie has revealed that the song's title and theme came to her and her brother while watching the BBC TV series *Sherlock*. The villain, Moriarty, says "In a world of locked rooms, the man with the key is king. And honey, you should see me in a crown." Apparently, both Billie and Finneas thought this sounded very "jiggy," and decided to write a song based on the line.

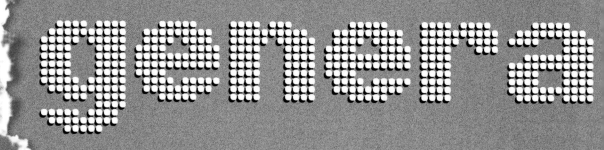

genera

Rising to fame as a teenager, Billie is the same age as many of her fans, and the responsibility of being their idol and the influence she possesses isn't lost on her. But ultimately, the message Billie tries to send out is that you have to remain true to yourself, "When you're looked up to as a role model, you can't let that change the way that you live," she said. The pop prodigy tries to avoid filtering herself and changing the way she acts to please other people. Her fearless determination to be exactly herself is one of the most inspiring things about Billie.

Full of empathy and apathy, Billie's musical melodies flit between emotions, ever-changing and evolving with the singer's own mood. Her songs are the sort of "alt-pop" that you can't tie down. Fierce, fearless, and full of personality, Billie's eclectic collection of songs span numerous thoughts and feelings unique to the young artist.

:ion girl

time to listen

As well as sharing her own thoughts and feelings, Billie is aware of the importance of reaching out to others and listening. "It doesn't make you weak to ask for help," she said. "It doesn't make you weak to ask for a friend, to go to a therapist. It shouldn't make you feel weak to ask anyone for help."

Billie has also shared how important it is to reach out to friends, "The main thing I'm trying to say is that you should keep your ears open and you should listen . . . even if it's just a little more comfort. That can really mean a lot to someone, because you don't know what is going on."

GIRL POWER

"THERE ARE STILL PEOPLE WHO ARE AFRAID OF SUCCESSFUL WOMEN."
—BILLIE EILISH

Billie doesn't fall into the media's idea of "It Girl" or "Pop Princess." She's unique and she's not afraid to tell people that. Billie has become an icon for a new generation and she is a powerful figure for those in the music and dance industries. Billie uses her position as a celebrity as a platform to inspire young people, especially young women wishing to pursue a career in the entertainment industry.

Having always been encouraged to be true to herself when she was growing up, Billie is not afraid to voice her opinions in public and to the media. She has often criticized the music industry and the media for their treatment of young women, "In the public eye, girls and women with strong perspectives are hated. If you're a girl with an opinion, people just hate you. There are still people who are afraid of successful women, and that's so lame."

Billie has called out the double standards women face in the music industry, and how, because of her gender, people feel like they have a right to comment on her lifestyle and appearance. "If I was a guy and I was wearing these baggy clothes, nobody would bat an eye. There's people out there saying, 'Dress like a girl for once! Wear tight clothes, you'd be much prettier and your career would be so much better!' No it wouldn't. It literally would not," she said.

smile for the camera

Billie has been criticized for never smiling in photographs. She has responded by saying that she does not like smiling because it makes her feel weak and powerless. But she says, "In real life, I'm a really smiley person. I smile when I talk and I laugh."

NO TIME FOR HATERS

> "PEOPLE UNDERESTIMATE THE POWER OF A YOUNG MIND."

While Billie has an insane following on social media, she actually has a love/hate relationship with the platforms and has warned other people about the dangers of using social media sites. She explained her feelings in an interview, "I love it and I hate it. Social media can ruin something. It can completely ruin a relationship, a friendship, yourself. It can ruin how you feel or how you feel like you look. I feel like social media is insanely dangerous."

Negative comments on her social media (she currently has over 20 million followers on Instagram and over two million on Twitter) keep her out off these social platforms. "I just don't wanna see all the horrible things people say." she said.

But the negativity has not kept her from using her platform for change and inspiring young people. Billie calls for people to be mindful of their behavior online, but still encourages them to share their opinions and passions.

young voices

As an icon for her generation, Billie is in a prominent position to share the opinions of young people across the world. Encouraging her young fans to raise their voices and actively protest for change, Billie has criticized older generations for refusing to listen. "People underestimate the power of a young mind that is new to everything and experiencing for the first time," she argued. "We're being ignored and it's so dumb. We know everything."

SING
HEART

Billie's songs are always a mood. Can you match the lyric with the song? Draw a line to connect each of the songs, and then check your answers.

1. I wanna make 'em scared like I could be anywhere

2. If teardrops could be bottled, there'd be swimming pools filled by models

3. Don't be cautious, don't be kind
You committed, I'm your crime ♫

4. Can't stop thinking of your diamond mind

YOUR
OUT

A. COPYCAT

B. bellyache

C. Ocean Eyes

D. idontwannabe-youanymore

1—B. 2—D. 3—A. 4—C

OSC in lyrics

"THERE ARE ALWAYS GOING TO BE BAD THINGS. BUT YOU CAN WRITE IT DOWN AND MAKE A SONG OUT OF IT."

_____

_____

_____

_____

_____

_____

_____

_____

_____

_____

_____

_____

_____

_____

_____

USE THE WORDS ON THIS PAGE TO INSPIRE YOU!

LOVE

hate

power

STRENGTH

high

LOW

PARTY

dreams

PERFORMANCE POWER

If all the world's a stage, then everyone has their eyes on Billie Eilish. From SoundCloud to Coachella, Billie has set her own path to become a generational icon.

Billie isn't your stereotypical pop diva, but she also isn't a gritty, in-your-face rapper. Billie's performance style is just as unique as her music. She creates a moment, an experience, a memory—it's something every fan in the crowd can get involved in, and this is an important part of every performance. "I don't want people at my shows to come out and say, 'I just saw a cool show.' I want them to say, 'I had fun at the show.' I want it to be a collaborative thing and be part of the audience and have them be part of me. I try to interact with everyone there and have them be equal to me, because they are."

"I LOVE PEOPLE TALKING ABOUT ME; I LOVE ANYBODY JUST LOOKING AT ME."

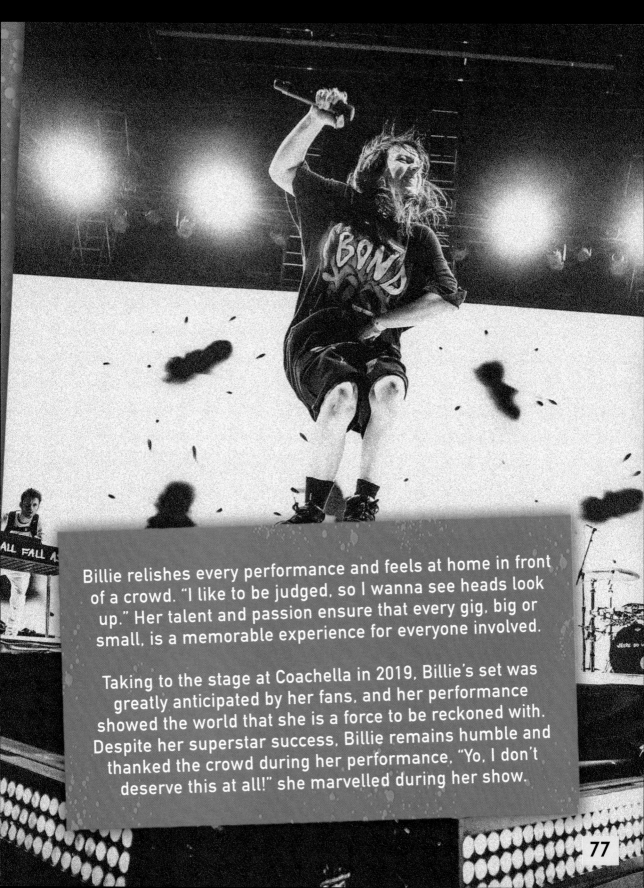

Billie relishes every performance and feels at home in front of a crowd. "I like to be judged, so I wanna see heads look up." Her talent and passion ensure that every gig, big or small, is a memorable experience for everyone involved.

Taking to the stage at Coachella in 2019, Billie's set was greatly anticipated by her fans, and her performance showed the world that she is a force to be reckoned with. Despite her superstar success, Billie remains humble and thanked the crowd during her performance, "Yo, I don't deserve this at all!" she marvelled during her show.

just be you

just be you

just be you

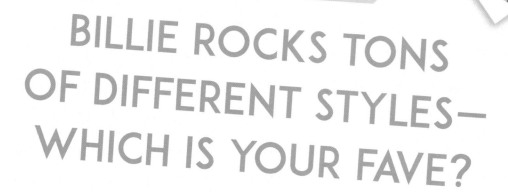

BILLIE ROCKS TONS OF DIFFERENT STYLES— WHICH IS YOUR FAVE?

NOW DESIGN YOUR VERY OWN AWESOME OUTFIT INSPIRED BY YOUR INDIVIDUAL STYLE.

dance ar

"ASIDE FROM SINGING, I'M ALSO A DANCER. I'VE BEEN DANCING SINCE I WAS 8."

Before she started her career as a pop star, Billie's first passion was for dance. When she was young, she was interested in contemporary dance and she would often be in the dance studio for up to eleven hours a week practicing her routines.

Billie's dance instructor was impressed by her talent and suggested a way for Billie to push things even further by incorporating her songwriting talent into her dancing. Without the encouragement from her dance instructor, Billie might never have pursued a career in singing or songwriting. Billie's dance instructor encouraged her to submit a song for class. As a result, Billie and her brother created the song that propelled her forward into the spotlight, "Ocean Eyes."

FLUID FEELINGS

Mixing dance with her music in an important part of Billie's unique style. She reflects her inner emotions through her lyrics, but also incorporates her passion for dance into her music. Billie performs in her music videos and physically expresses the lyrics she writes through her movement.

DANCING DANGERS

In 2016, Billie suffered a dance injury when she was dancing with some of the older performers in her class. Her bone separated from her hip muscle after she was doing some hip-hop moves and her bone popped.

you-nique
you-nique

Busy schedules, around-the-world tours, and regular rehearsals can be super tiring, so it's important for Billie to have other things in her life that help her to wind down. Just like her music, Billie's favorite things are unique to her.

you-nique
you-nique
you-nique
you-nique
you-nique
you-nique

FAVORITE COLOR:
Yellow

FAVORITE FASHION BRANDS:
Gucci, Fendi, Golf Wang, and Off-White

FAVORITE MOVIE:
Billie has a thing for horror. She explained that one of her favorite horror movie is *The Babadook.*

FAVORITE TV SERIES:
The Walking Dead, American Horror Story

CREEPY CREATIONS

Billie's first song was about zombies. Billie started writing songs when she was 11 years old. It was a way for her to express her thoughts. In an interview she explained that her first real composition was inspired by the popular zombie TV show, *The Walking Dead.*

"It's called "Fingers Crossed." I literally just watched *The Walking Dead* and I took little lines from it. Just watch all of *The Walking Dead* and you'll find some things that are in my song and some episode titles that are in my song."

ARE YOU FOR REAL?

You're obsessed with Billie's songs and unique style, but how well do you really know her? Take this quiz and find out how much you really know about music's bad girl.

1. WHEN IS HER BIRTHDAY?

A. December 18, 2001

B. November 18, 1999

C. March 30, 2004

D. October 30, 2003

2. WHEN DID SHE START DANCING?

A. 8 years old

B. 2 years old

C. 1 month old

D. 3 years old

3. BILLIE OFTEN WORKS WITH HER BROTHER ON THE MUSIC SHE MAKES. WHAT IS HER BROTHER'S NAME?

A. Tyler James Eilish

B. Finneas O'Connell

C. Thomas Iwan O'Connell

D. Danny Eilish

4. WHICH BAND DID HER BROTHER, FINNEAS, PLAY IN?

A. Rookies

B. The Slightlys

C. The Faintlys

D. Superheroes

5. WHAT YEAR DID BILLIE RELEASE HER HIT SINGLE "OCEAN EYES" THROUGH INTERSCOPE RECORDS (NOT THE SOUNDCLOUD VERSION)?

A. 2016   **B. 2017**   **C. 2018**

9. WHICH SERIES ON NETFLIX HAS FEATURED BILLIE'S SONG "LOVELY" ON THE SOUNDTRACK?

A. *Riverdale*

B. 13 Reasons Why

C. Chilling Adventures of Sabrina

D. Stranger Things

wise words

TAKE SOME ADVICE FROM BILLIE AND STAY TRUE TO YOURSELF.

"I'VE ALWAYS DONE WHATEVER I WANT AND ALWAYS BEEN EXACTLY WHO I AM."

"I'M SUPER SELF-CRITICAL, WHICH I THINK IS GOOD, BECAUSE THEN I GET EXACTLY WHAT I WANT."

"I'M GONNA MAKE WHAT I WANT TO MAKE, AND OTHER PEOPLE ARE GONNA LIKE WHAT THEY'RE GONNA LIKE. IT DOESN'T REALLY MATTER."

"IT DOESN'T MAKE YOU WEAK TO ASK FOR HELP."

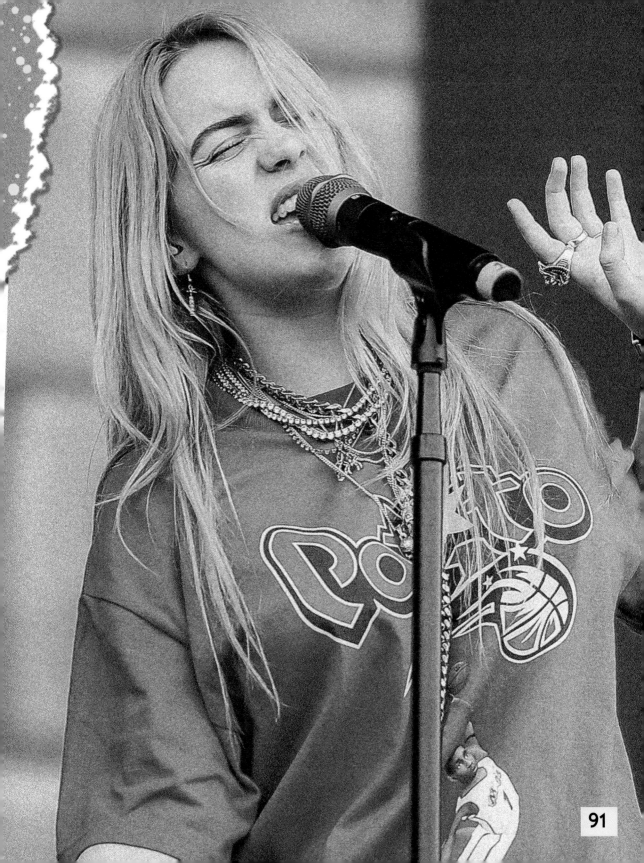

TAKE

LEAP

So you've reached the end of the book—and you're probably feeling inspired by how passionate, talented, and empowering Billie is. Take in some last words of wisdom from the musical megastar, and then plan your own amazing goals for the future.

"I'm trying to show everybody that I'm a girl, and I'm five foot four, and you can do anything you want, no matter your gender. It's your world, too!"

HOW ARE YOU GOING TO TAKE THE FIRST STEPS TOWARD FOLLOWING YOUR DREAMS?

Today I will. . .

_____

_____

_____

This week I will. . .

_____

_____

_____

This year I will. . .

_____

_____

_____

PICTURE CREDITS